Published 2021
Little Brother Books Ltd, Ground Floor, 23 Southernhay East, Exeter, Devon, EX1 1QL
Printed in Turkey.
books@littlebrotherbooks.co.uk
www.littlebrotherbooks.co.uk

D0493301

LB LittleBrother BOOKS

MINECRAFT: GET STARTED

New to Minecraft and looking for some guidance? We're here to help!

BLOCKS

Everything in Minecraft is made of blocks! That can mean a block of dirt or stone, or a block of air or water! There are hundreds to find, and they all have their own special properties. Most can be created or destroyed one way or another. When you hit a block, you'll see it slowly start to crack, and it will either break, meaning it disappears completely, or drop, which is when you can collect it.

ITEMS

Some blocks drop items, which are things that interact with blocks. A pickaxe, for example, is used to mine specific blocks faster, or to make them drop instead of break. Coal ore drops the item coal when mined. The only difference is that items can't be placed permanently in the world – they spin slowly on the ground until collected, or until they despawn (disappear forever).

MOBS

Mobs – short for "mobiles" – means anything in the world that is alive. The Player (that's you!) is a mob, and so are all the bad guys you encounter, from the infamous creeper to the terrifying ender dragon. Peaceful animals like chickens, pigs and cows are also mobs, as are villagers! All mobs have health, and they usually drop something when they're killed, whether that's an item or just experience points.

TIP: The entire world is generated based on a seed every time you create a new map, so no two maps are the same unless you use the same seed!

CRAFTING

Combining blocks and items into other blocks and items is called "crafting", and you can do this in various ways. We'll cover the easiest later on! Just be aware that crafting can refer to lots of different activities, including smelting ore, cooking food or creating a map.

INVENTORY

Your inventory is where you keep things you've collected, and there are a few types of inventory! Your quickbar is always visible, and a space for the items you'll need most often. The highlighted slot matches the item currently in your hand. You also have extra space in your pockets. Each of these slots can contain a stack of items and blocks, and the stack size depends on the object type. Dirt and stone stack in groups of up to 64, whereas tools and armour can't stack at all. You also have four inventory slots for armour/clothes, and a final slot for your "offhand", which is usually dormant but can be quickly swapped into the main hand!

HEALTH, HUNGER & EXPERIENCE

You need to keep track of three progress bars. The green experience bar fills up by killing mobs, collecting ore or cooking food, and this experience can be "spent" on advanced crafting activities. The health bar shows you how hurt you are. If you die, you drop all of your items, lose all your health, and return to the spawn point. The hunger bar empties over time and can be replenished by eating. When it's full your health starts to refill, and when it's low you'll lose the ability to sprint.

TIP: Every time your experience bar fills up, you'll gain a level, which is reduced when you spend experience.

THE IDEAL
SHELTER

When you arrive in Minecraft, the first thing you need to do is build a safe haven before night falls...

STEP ONE:
COLLECT BLOCKS

Wherever you start in the Overworld, there will be blocks to collect. Trees are fairly easy to break and wood is very versatile, so you should start by punching some tree trunks. These blocks will drop as logs. When you have a few, open your inventory and move them into the 2x2 crafting grid. You'll see from the output slot to the right of it that each log can be crafted into four blocks of wood planks. You can also craft two planks into four sticks, and four planks into a crafting table. Now we can really get started!

STEP TWO:
CRAFT GEAR

Place the crafting table you just made into the world, then open up the crafting interface. You need to craft a few pieces of gear, including a pickaxe (*two sticks, three planks*), a shovel (*two sticks, one plank*) and an axe (*two sticks, three planks*). Wood tools are the most basic, but still faster than doing things by hand.

The goal now is to gather wood and stone to build your shelter. Look out for coal ore, too, to craft torches. You should find this stuff close by, but once it gets dark hostile mobs start spawning, so you have about 10 minutes from the moment you enter the game.

TIP: If you're caught out by the night, your axe will do lots of damage to mobs (but swords are faster and less quick to break).

CRAFT GEAR

ADD FURNITURE

STEP THREE:
BUILD THE SHELTER

Once you've collected enough wood or cobblestone, mark out a decent-sized perimeter on the ground and quickly build it up to a three-block height. For now, just make sure there's a nice, flat floor and a two-block high space for the door. Add a roof using any type of block: cobblestone looks bad but is very strong; planks look good but are flammable!

Remember that whatever you build now doesn't have to last forever. You can replace materials, extend the house, or even abandon it. Having a safe spot to return to early on is the purpose of your first shelter.

STEP FOUR:
ADD FURNITURE

Once the roof is on, move the crafting table inside, place a door (*six planks*) in the gap you left, then light the interior with torches (*one coal and one stick*). When night falls, your fully lit shelter will be safe from mobs whilst the door is shut.

As you wait out the night, craft a furnace (*eight cobblestone*) for smelting/cooking, and a couple of chests (*eight planks each*) to store your stuff. If you're REALLY lucky, you'll spawn near some sheep – kill three to get the wool for a bed (*three planks and three wool*). When you sleep in the bed, it will set your spawn point there AND skip the night!

TIP: Build your first shelter close to your initial spawn point so you don't lose track of it when you die!

ORE: A SPOTTER'S GUIDE

Here's what to look out for every time you hit the mines!

COAL

Coal ore generates in the Overworld wherever stone is found, meaning you can find it underground and even high up in cliffs. It can be mined with a wooden pickaxe (or better) and will drop one piece of coal per block mined. The coal can then be used to craft torches, or as fuel in furnaces.

IRON

Iron ore is found in layers 0-64 of the Overworld, so you have to look underground for it! It drops itself when mined with a stone pickaxe (or better), but you can then smelt the ore into an ingot using a furnace. You can use the iron in many recipes, but most usefully for making iron tools and armour!

GOLD

Gold ore is quite rare and found in layers 0-34 of the Overworld, but mostly below layer 29! In the Badlands biome, it can also generate on the surface (up to layer 80), especially in the abandoned mines that appear there. You need an iron pickaxe (or better) to mine gold ore, which, again, can be smelted into gold ingots for use in crafting.

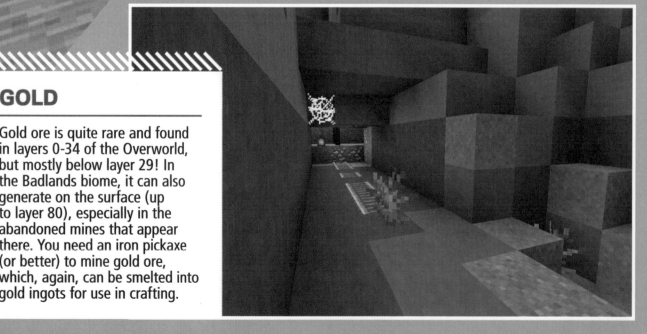

COAL, IRON, GOLD AND DIAMOND

DIAMOND AND REDSTONE

LAPIS LAZULI

This mineral ore generates in layers 0-34 and can be mined with a stone pickaxe (or better). When mined, it drops 4-9 pieces of lapis lazuli, which can be crafted into dye or used to power enchantments.

REDSTONE

Redstone ore generates in the same places as diamond ore, but is much more common. It can be mined with an iron pickaxe (or better) and will drop 4-5 piles of redstone dust, for crafting redstone items or laying redstone wires on the ground. When struck, redstone ore emits a dim light for a short time.

EMERALD

Emerald ore is found only in the Mountains biome in single blocks! It generates in layers 0-33 and can be mined with an iron pickaxe (or better). It's the rarest ore in the Overworld and drops just one emerald when mined. Emeralds can be crafted into decorative blocks, but are more popular for use as money, as you can trade them with villagers to get rare and useful items!

TIP: Those blocks you crafted before? You can turn them back into ingots or gems by putting them on a crafting table!

DIAMOND

Diamond ore is rare, found in layers 0-20 of the Overworld, so very deep underground. You can use an iron pickaxe (or better) to mine it, and an ore block will drop one diamond when mined. Diamonds are also best used for crafting gear!

TIP: You can usually combine ingots, gems and coal into solid blocks by crafting nine of them together!

COPPER

Copper was added in version 1.17, and copper ore generates anywhere iron forms. It also works in the same way – you need a stone pickaxe (or better) to mine it and you can smelt the ore into ingots. Copper blocks will tarnish when placed, turning from bronze to green!

EMERALD ORE

CRAFT THE BEST GEAR

Now you know how to craft AND how to find ore, here's what you need to make the best tools...

MATERIALS

Tools and weapons can (mostly) be crafted out of various different materials. The material an item is made of can determine its speed, durability and enchantability. Here's how the differing materials stack up, listed from worst to best:

SPEED: Wood, stone, iron, diamond, Netherite, gold
DURABILITY: Gold, wood, stone, iron, diamond, Netherite
ENCHANTABILITY: Stone, diamond, iron, wood/Netherite, gold
DAMAGE: Wood/gold, stone, iron, diamond, Netherite

What you can learn from this, for example, is that gold makes for very weak tools that fall apart fast, but they can work quickly and provide the highest enchantments. Iron, meanwhile, is a good all-rounder, but maybe not the best choice when it comes to enchanting!

DURABILITY POINTS

Each time you use a tool or weapon, it loses a point of durability, and for some uses it may lose two points. When the durability drops to zero, the tool will break. You can repair and combine two unenchanted items of the same type on a crafting grid or an anvil. This combines their remaining durability points and adds a 5% bonus.

TIP: Iron is common and great for everything but taking enchantments, so make most of your gear out of it early on!

WEAPONS

DURABILITY POINTS

TOOLS

TOOLS

The list of tools is long, but here are some of the most important!

PICKAXE (*two sticks and three materials*): Mines stone blocks more quickly, and mines blocks so they drop instead of breaking.

SHOVEL (*two sticks and one material*): Mines dirt, sand and snow blocks faster. Can also flatten grass.

AXE (*two sticks and three materials*): Increases mining speed on wood blocks. Can be used to strip logs and as a weapon.

HOE (*two sticks and two materials*): Turns dirt blocks into farmland.

FLINT & STEEL (*one iron ingot and one flint*): Used to light fires.

SHEARS (*two iron ingots):* Shear sheep, and collect grass and leaves.

COMPASS (*four iron and one redstone):* Points back to the world spawn.

FISHING ROD (*three sticks and two string*): Allows you to catch fish in water.

SPYGLASS (*one amethyst shard and two copper ingots*): Lets you see over long distances.

WEAPONS

Swords (*two materials and one stick*) are the main melee weapon, and although axes may be stronger per hit, they lose durability faster and strike slower than swords.

You can also craft a bow (*three sticks and three string*) and arrows (*one feather, one stick, one flint*) for ranged attacks.

Later on, you'll find crossbows and tridents, which can be collected as drops. Crossbows can fire arrows more accurately, and tridents work well underwater.

TIP: You can use an anvil to repair items and weapons with their base material, so gold ingots can repair gold tools!

PROTECT

The best defence is... well, a good defence!

MATERIALS

Wearing armour protects you from damage and, like tools and weapons, it can be crafted from several different materials, although there are also some unique alternatives that we'll get to!
Here's how the options for standard armour stack up:

ARMOUR DURABILITY:
Leather, gold, chainmail, iron, diamond, Netherite
ARMOUR
ENCHANTABILITY: Iron, diamond, chainmail, leather/Netherite, gold
As with other items, it's possible to repair and combine partially used pieces of armour using a crafting grid or an anvil.

ARMOUR BAR

When you wear armour, you add an extra armour bar to your display, which shows you how much protection your combined suit of armour is offering. This protection will stay in effect until a piece of armour breaks by running out of durability. A full set of diamond or Netherite gear is required to fill your armour bar completely.

TURTLE SHELL

MATERIALS

PIECES OF ARMOUR

PUMPKIN

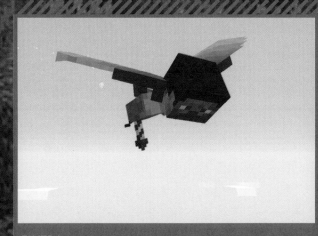

ELYTRA

PIECES OF ARMOUR

There are four pieces of armour: a helmet, a chestpiece, leggings and boots. If they're made of leather, these same pieces are called a cap, a tunic, pants and boots.

TIP: You can't craft chainmail armour – it's only available as treasure, through trading or as drops from mobs that spawn wearing it.

Alternative items you can wear in your armour slot include:

TURTLE SHELL

The turtle shell is crafted from five scutes, dropped when a turtle grows to adulthood. As well as providing protection equivalent to iron armour, it gives you the Water Breathing effect – an extra 10 seconds of air when underwater.

PUMPKIN

Carved pumpkins can be worn as helmets. They provide no protection and obscure your vision with a Jack o'lantern face. However, they allow you to look at endermen without provoking them and help you to avoid fights in the End.

MOB HEAD

Mob heads only drop when certain mobs are killed by charged creeper explosions, or you kill enough of them. They reduce the detection range for that mob, so if you wear a creeper head, creepers won't chase you until you're within eight blocks of them.

ELYTRA

The elytra are a pair of extendable wings that allow you to glide. You can only collect them from the End, and they're worn in the chestplate slot. Check out our guide to the End for more about how to find them!

TIP: You can use a lightning rod or Channeling-enchanted trident to make creating charged creepers a lot easier.

PROJECT #2 GROW YOUR OWN FOOD

It won't be long before you need your own food supply to sate your hunger…

STEP ONE: COLLECT STARTER SEEDS

Eating food refills your hunger bar, so you'll have to do it regularly, and the best way to do that is to make your own food. The first thing you need to begin planting crops is seeds. The easiest form of seeds to find are wheat, which you can get by breaking long grass (it occurs naturally in almost every biome). If you find a village with a farm, you can also scavenge potatoes, carrots and beetroot from it. These are the easiest crops to grow, as others, such as melons, pumpkins, cocoa beans and sugar cane, have extra requirements!

You won't need too many seeds to begin with. We'll assume you're growing wheat to make bread, so find a minimum of three sets of seeds to plant, but more isn't a bad idea!

STEP TWO: CREATE FARMLAND

Seeds must be planted in farmland to grow. Craft a hoe (*two sticks and two of any material*), then use it to turn dirt into farmland. If the farmland dries out, it will turn back into dirt, so make sure it's within three blocks of a water source block. If you craft a bucket (*three iron ingots*), you can collect water from a river or pond and use it to make some irrigation. When the farmland is wet, it turns a darker brown, signifying that it's ready for planting.

TIP: If you're looking for food but haven't got time to farm, scavenge apples by breaking oak leaf blocks.

CREATE FARMLAND

HARVEST

STEP THREE: GROW CROPS

Use the seeds on the farmland to plant them. They'll turn into small, green shoots, which grow over time in seven stages. It takes five to 35 minutes for a plant to grow to its final stage, and if it's harvested before then you'll only collect the seeds you planted.

Plants don't just need watering – they need light, too! They'll stop growing at night unless you put lights (like torches) nearby.

You can speed up the growth of crops by one stage if you fertilise them with bonemeal, crafted from bones (dropped by skeletons) or by filling up a composter (*seven wood slabs*) with compostable plant material.

STEP FOUR: HARVEST

Once a crop is fully grown, break it however you like. The block will drop enough crop to eat and some to plant again! Wheat drops a sheaf of wheat and up to three seeds. Carrots drop 2-4 carrots, so you can eat some and replant more.

Once collected, some food can be eaten directly (carrots, beetroots), some can be cooked (potatoes) and some can be crafted into other foods. Wheat is very versatile: three wheat make a loaf of bread, two wheat and one cocoa beans make cookies, and three wheat, an egg, two sugar (crafted from sugar cane) and three buckets of milk make a whole cake!

TIP: Fence off farmland to stop mobs walking over it at night, as this can destroy the farmland and uproot any unfinished crops!

LIGHT & WEATHER SECRETS

Whether it's day or night, sunny or raining, there's always stuff going on in Minecraft!

LIGHT LEVELS

Everything that emits light – including the sun – has a light level. The lowest is 0 (no light) and the highest is 15 (full daylight). If the light level in an area is 9 or below, it means mobs can spawn, which is why they come out at night and hide in caves. It also explains how they can stay alive in the shade of trees!

Torches emit a light level of 14 and are the easiest way to light a lot of space. You can also use other light-emitting blocks such as glowstone, sea lanterns, candles, lanterns, End rods and Jack o'lanterns. Some of these even work underwater, which is something torches can't do!

LIGHT SECRETS

Fire emits a light level of 15, but it can easily spread if not properly managed!

Zombies, phantoms and skeletons will burn in direct sunlight if the light level goes above 12.

In daylight, spiders and cave spiders will become passive and only attack if provoked.

Artificial light sources of level 11 or higher will melt any snow around them.

Crops will uproot if the light level is 7 or lower, and can only grow in light level 9 or higher. Mushrooms will uproot in light level 13 or higher, unless planted in podzol, mycelium or nylium.

TIP: The moon phase changes from one night to the next, but the fullness doesn't effect its brightness – it's always level 4.

LIGHT LEVELS

IT'S RAINING, IT'S POURING

ALL ABOUT WEATHER

ALL ABOUT WEATHER

There are three states for weather: Clear is the default setting; Rain means rain will fall and the sky darkens; Thunder is a Minecraft storm. Here, the sky darkens even more, to the point where mobs can spawn in the day, and lightning strikes will hit the ground.

The weather in the Overworld is the same everywhere. The End and the Nether don't have weather!

Sleep in a bed to skip rain, snow or thunder.

MOBS & WEATHER

IT'S RAINING, IT'S POURING

Rain falls as snow in cold biomes, or at high altitudes, depositing snow layers on the ground. It never rains in hot biomes, such as deserts, Badlands and savanna!

A lightning rod can be used to attract lightning strikes. It will prevent a fire forming wherever lightning strikes, and emit a redstone signal that can be used to trigger a circuit.

Rain puts out any fires that aren't burning on Netherrack.

MOBS & WEATHER

Lightning strikes can transform certain mobs. A creeper struck by lightning will become a powerful charged creeper. A villager becomes a witch, a pig becomes a piglin, and a mooshroom becomes a brown mooshroom. A turtle struck by lightning will drop a bowl!

When it's raining, mobs hurt by water – endermen, striders and blazes, for example – will take damage.

TIP: If it's raining, you can use the Channeling enchantment on a trident to summon lightning, or the Riptide enchantment to travel to wherever the trident is thrown.

MOB DROPS

Grab your sword and start collecting some rewards!

EXPERIENCE

Almost every mob you kill will drop useful items when you dispatch it. Most drop experience points, and killing mobs is the quickest way to gain experience levels. These appear in the form of glowing yellow and green orbs, which creep slowly towards you when you're close. Generally, neutral and friendly mobs offer 3-5 experience points, and hostile mobs give 7-15. The amount of experience a mob drops is increased if they're wearing equipment, so a skeleton with a full set of armour is worth more experience than a normal one.

EXPERIENCE

EQUIPMENT

If a mob is wearing armour or carrying an item, there's a small chance they'll drop that item when killed. The chance of dropping an item is 12.5%, so about one in every eight kills. The equipment dropped by mobs is normally worn, so might require repair, but there's also a good chance of it being enchanted, so look out!

HOSTILE MOBS

There are too many drops to list every kind here, but some are worth keeping an eye out for early on!
    Skeletons drop arrows, which you can use as ammo in a bow or crossbow, and bones, which can be crafted into bonemeal fertiliser.
    Creepers drop gunpowder, which can be used to craft TNT or fireworks.
    Spiders drop string, which you can craft as part of bows, fishing rods, leads, or even into wool!

TIP: Not every mob drop is the same every time. Adult horses can drop 0-2 pieces of leather, so you might not always get some, but you'll always get experience!

NEUTRAL MOBS

It's possible to breed neutral mobs by finding two of the same kind and feeding them the right food (e.g. feeding seeds to chickens, or wheat to cows). This means you can grow a herd of animals, and farm the items they drop. When mobs breed, they spawn a baby mob, which won't drop any items or experience if killed. If you're planning to farm them, you need to wait until they're grown-up to collect the drops, which takes about 10 minutes!

FOOD

NEUTRAL MOBS

RARE DROPS

FOOD

Most neutral mobs drop food items which, when cooked, restore more health than most. You can cook food drops in a furnace, a smoker or around a campfire. Cooked steaks are some of the best food you can eat, and breeding cows will allow you to collect lots of steak and leather! As well as dropping a raw chicken and feathers when killed, chickens lay eggs – around one every 5-10 minutes. Eggs can't be eaten directly, but they can be crafted as part of cakes. You can also throw an egg for a chance to spawn a baby chicken!

RARE DROPS

Rare drops are single items that only occur in some circumstances. Only one in 10 rabbits will drop a rabbit's foot when killed. About one in 15 drowned will drop a gold ingot. One in 40 wither skeletons drop a wither skeleton skull, and zombies have a one in 40 chance of dropping an iron ingot, a carrot or a potato! If you trick a skeleton into killing a creeper with an arrow, the creeper will drop a music disc!

TIP: If you kill a neutral mob by setting it on fire, it may drop cooked meat rather than the raw type – so no need to cook it!

ADVANCED MAP MAKING

Keep track of your explorations with a map!

CRAFTING A MAP

Making a map is simple: you just need a compass (*one redstone dust and four iron*) and eight sheets of paper (*three pieces of sugar cane per sheet*). To fill in the map, select it in your inventory and click use. The map will fill up with everything around you, and as you walk around the map will fill up until it's complete. The white dot on the map? That's you! If you make any changes in the world, the map will update if you walk near the same area while holding it.

MAP SCALE

The first map you make has a scale that isn't particularly useful: one block in the world is one pixel on the map. To change the scale, put the map in the centre of a crafting table and surround it with paper. The next time you look at it, you'll see that you have a new map with a slightly larger scale. You can do this four times to the same map. The smallest maps show 128 blocks square, while the largest cover 2048 blocks square!

COPYING MAPS

You can share maps with other players to allow them to see the areas you've explored. Better still, if you copy it, they can help you fill it in, too! In the Java Edition, you can copy a map by crafting it with an empty map. On the Bedrock Edition, you have to do the same but with an anvil.

TIP: Put a map in your offhand slot to view it as a minimap on your screen at all times!

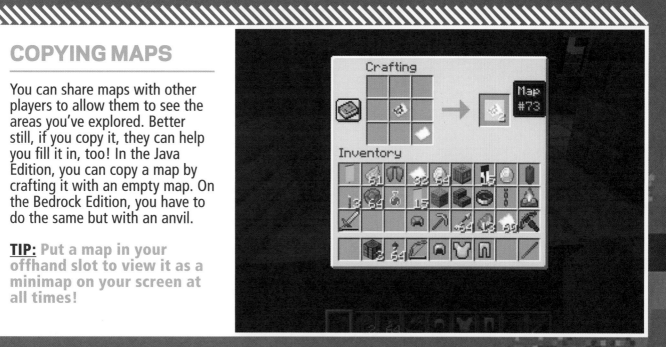

FRAMING MAPS

If you craft an item frame (*one leather surrounded by eight sticks*), you can place the frame on a wall, then put a map in it. If the maps are the same scale, they'll line up to create one large, unbroken map.

NAMED MARKERS

On the Java Edition, you can place a marker on a map. If you put a banner (*one stick and six wool*) in the world, you can use a map on it to put a permanent pin on the map, which will appear in the banner's base wool colour. If you use an anvil to rename the banner, when you use the map on it the name also appears on the map. In this way, you can name locations and set reminders!

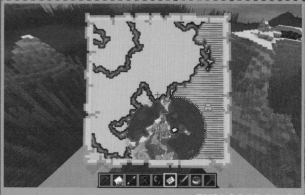

EXPLORER MAP

EXPLORER MAPS

If you find a map as loot or buy one from a cartographer villager, you might have an explorer map! Explorer maps show the location of mansions, buried treasure and ocean monuments, initially as a rough location that fills in with detail as you get closer to it. The nearer you get, the more accurate they are, so check them regularly – and remember, if you're looking for treasure, x marks the spot.

TIP: If the white blob is at the edge of the map, it means you're off the edge of it – useful to know when you're trying to fill in explorer maps!

FRAMING MAPS

ENCHANT YOUR GEAR

Upgrade your tools, weapons and armour with enchantments!

STEP ONE:
COLLECT YOUR MATERIALS

You'll need the following to craft the enchanting table:
> Two diamond (mined from diamond ore)
> One book (crafted from one leather and three paper, obtained by trading, or collected as loot)
> Three obsidian (mined from obsidian blocks with a diamond pickaxe)

To make bookshelves, you'll need three books and six wood planks per bookshelf. If you're crafting this from scratch, you'll need to collect leather from cows and horses, and paper from three pieces of sugar cane. It's also possible to collect books from library village buildings, and paper from cartographer houses, so there are shortcuts!

Finally, you need lapis lazuli – at least one piece per enchantment you wish to make, but get as much as possible!

STEP TWO: CRAFT AN ENCHANTING STATION

To enchant gear, you first need to craft an enchanting table and set it up in a safe place.

Once placed, enchanting tables can be optionally "powered up" with bookshelves. Placing them around the table, as shown below, gives you access to more powerful and higher-level enchantments. The maximum number of bookshelves you can use to raise the enchantment level is 15, and there must be nothing between the table and the bookshelf for it to affect the enchanting table!

TIP: Don't like the enchantments on offer? Place blocks between the table and bookshelves to change and reshuffle the levels!

CRAFT AN ENCHANTING STATION

ENJOY YOUR ENCHANTED GEAR

STEP THREE: PUT GEAR ON THE TABLE

When you open the enchanting table interface, you'll see two input slots: one is for the item you wish to enchant. Most tools, weapons and armour can be enchanted, as well as books. Books tend to take lower enchantments than items, but this allows you to create a library of enchantments ready for when you have an item you want a specific enchantment on.

In the second slot, you need to put a piece of lapis lazuli. This will be consumed if you choose the first, second or third enchantment in the list on the right, along with a number of experience levels. So all that's left to do now is choose an enchantment!

STEP TWO: ENJOY YOUR ENCHANTED GEAR

Every piece of gear has a number of enchantments that can be suggested, but you won't be able to guess exactly which ones are being offered. You might want to enchant a book instead, to avoid adding an enchantment you don't want to a treasured piece of gear!

The enchantment will be applied as soon as you select it, and the required amount of experience and lapis will be spent.

TIP: "Treasure enchantments" can't be conjured up on an enchanting table – Frost Walker, for example, is only available as loot!

TRADING WITH VILLAGERS

Is crafting too much effort? Try trading instead!

CURRENCY

Almost all adult villagers allow you to trade with them: by exchanging emeralds, or by trading goods directly. You can get emeralds by mining them from ore, collecting them as treasure or loot, or by selling unwanted goods to the right villager (e.g. paper to a cartographer).

VILLAGER PROFESSIONS

A villager's profession decides what they can trade, and their profession can be determined from their outfit. A farmer will buy crops and sell food items, and wears a straw hat. Weaponsmiths have eyepatches, armourers have a welding mask, and librarians have glasses. There are 13 professions in total, plus the nitwit who has no profession. Not every village has every type of profession in it, so note which ones contain which jobs!

CURRENCY

PROFESSIONS

TRADING RANKS

When you trade with a villager, their experience will increase, potentially raising their rank and unlocking extra, better trades. The rank is shown by the badge on their outfit. A stone badge indicates a novice, an iron badge indicates an apprentice, a gold badge indicates a journeyman, an emerald badge indicates an expert, and a diamond badge indicates a master.

TIP: Villager professions are tied to their utility blocks, so a nitwit can use an unclaimed cartography table to become a cartographer, for example.

TRADE OFFERINGS

If you want to see trades from multiple villagers at once, you can make a "trade offering", which involves standing where several villagers can see you and holding the item you wish to trade (e.g. an emerald). Villagers who want the item will walk up to you and cycle through the items they're willing to trade, allowing you to quickly see what's on offer. When you know what you want, you can open the normal trading interface with that villager. It's especially useful if you have multiple villagers of the same type in a village, who may have different offers to trade!

WANDERING TRADERS

If you see a blue-robed villager travelling around with two llamas, then good news! You've bumped into a wandering trader. These have a one in 13 chance of appearing randomly in the Overworld once every 20 minutes, and do so within a 48-block range of the player. They'll then despawn after 40-60 minutes of wandering around. Wandering traders never buy items off the player and carry six random items, five of which are common and one of which is rare. Common items include flowers and plants, sand, pumpkins, sea pickles, glowstone, kelp, coral blocks, cactus blocks, slimeballs and nautilus shells. Rare items include gunpowder, podzol, packed ice, pufferfish/ tropical fish bucket and blue ice. These items aren't especially useful, but they do allow you to collect many blocks that might otherwise only be available in a distant biome.

TIP: If you want, you can kill the wandering trader's llamas and collect the leads – items that are quite rare!

TRADE OFFERINGS

TRADING RANKS

WANDERING TRADERS

TEMPLES
STEP-BY-STEP

Have you found a temple? Here's how to get the loot inside...

JUNGLE TEMPLES

These three-floored structures are built of cobblestone and appear in most jungles. Inside, a puzzle leads to two chests containing useful loot like diamonds, saddles, emeralds, books and horse armour, but you'll have to avoid the traps to get them!

To get through a jungle temple safely, make sure you bring a pair of shears! Enter the temple from the roof and travel to the lowest floor. At the bottom, check whether there are levers to your left or right. If the levers are on the left, hit them in the order R L L R. If they're on the right, hit them L R R L. This will open a secret door to reveal the first chest. Turn around the corner, cutting the tripwire as you pass. At the end of the hall is a second chest – cut a tripwire in front of it to get the loot!

DESERT TEMPLES

JUNGLE TEMPLES

DESERT TEMPLES

These pyramid-like buildings appear in deserts and may be buried in sand. Each one has a large pit laced with TNT, which hides four treasure chests containing saddles, emeralds, diamonds, horse armour and more!

To dig safely to the chests, stand in the temple doorway, face the blue clay block and begin to dig a stairway down until you break into the main pit. Quickly place some torches so that the light stops mobs spawning and setting off the trap, then make your way to the bottom where you can break the pressure plate with a pickaxe. Easy!

TIP: You can loot the arrows from dispensers in a jungle temple – not to mention the dispensers themselves!

STRONGHOLDS
STEP-BY-STEP

These huge underground dungeons are rare - and hide a secret...

LOCATING STRONGHOLDS

Found underground, it's very difficult to break into a stronghold on luck alone. Instead, you have to get an eye of ender (craft an ender pearl with blaze powder) and throw it to find the direction you should travel. Eyes of ender break after a few uses, so you'll need several to get started! Eventually, the eye will hover in place instead of heading away from you, and that's when you need to start digging to find the stronghold.

LAYOUT

Strongholds are huge mazes of rooms and repeating features, so mapping them out is very difficult. Look out for libraries and store rooms, which are good places to find chests and bookshelves, and contain plenty of loot. Eventually, if you're lucky, you'll come across a portal room. This contains a portal to the End, of which you can learn more about later on!

SURVIVAL TACTICS

Many of the stone brick blocks in strongholds hide silverfish eggs, so try to avoid breaking anything. Make sure you keep track of where you've been (by putting down markers of some kind) to avoid getting lost and help guide you towards unexplored parts, where yet more loot might be found! Don't be afraid to set up a small safe zone to return to – if you die and lose your stuff, it might never be found again!

TIP: Not every stronghold has a portal room because caves and other underground features can cut them off. But don't worry, there are other strongholds out there.

LOCATING STRONGHOLDS

LAYOUT

SURVIVAL TACTICS

MONUMENTS
STEP-BY-STEP

Ocean monuments are one of the hardest challenges!

LOCATING

Monuments only generate in Deep Ocean biomes and are entirely submerged in water, making it difficult to survive inside them. Built from prismarine and lit by sea lanterns, they're surrounded by dangerous fish-like enemies known as guardians. You can either use an explorer map to find one, or craft a boat and go searching.

EXPLORING

The elder guardian boss will inflict you with the Mining Fatigue effect, so breaking in and out of monuments is nearly impossible. Build a base nearby with an air pocket, then set a spawn point there by sleeping in a bed. You'll die quite often! Fill up on potions, food, weapons and armour. A turtle helmet enchanted with Respiration III will give you 55 extra seconds of air underwater, Depth Strider boots stop you from slowing down in water, and a trident is essential!

INSIDE

The interior of a monument is full of water, so it's difficult enough to survive without guardians attacking you! Invisibility potions and ender pearls will help you sneak inside, and remember to create safe havens and airlocks so you can replenish your air levels. Guardian attacks are hard to avoid, so get in and out quickly and heal regularly. When you find the elder guardian, wear down its health slowly. The large pillar it guards hides four solid blocks of gold – your prize for defeating the monument!

TIP: Look out for sponges! You can get one per ender guardian you kill, or collect them from a sponge room. They don't appear anywhere else!

LOCATING

EXPLORING

INSIDE

MANSIONS
STEP-BY-STEP

Vast and dangerous, mansions are great fun to explore!

FINDING MANSIONS

Woodland mansions only appear in the Dark Forest biome, and are difficult to find without an explorer map bought from a Journeyman-level cartographer. There's no mistaking when you see one, though, as they're massive and several times taller than the forest around them! Mansios have three floors and the entrance is on the ground one, although that doesn't mean you can't break in from the top, too.

WHAT YOU'LL FIND

Inside a mansion is a snaking corridor that leads around the building. Off this hallway, you'll find tens of different rooms in a randomly generated layout. The mobs inside are particularly dangerous – vindicators, as well as creepers and skeletons – so it's not for the novice! If you beat the boss mob – the evoker – you'll receive a totem of undying, which brings you back to life if you're holding it in your hand when you die. There are other loot chests to find, as well as lots of rare and useful blocks. Make sure you have loads of spare space to carry stuff!

SECRET ROOMS

Some rooms aren't connected to the main corridor, so remember to try breaking down a wall if you think there's space for a room but no way in. There are eight different secret rooms in total, and most contain something useful, like diamond, enchanted gear, chests and more!

TIP: Fifty-two different types of room can appear in a mansion. Eight of them are secret, and 11 contain loot chests of some kind.

FINDING MANSIONS

WHAT YOU'LL FIND

SECRET ROOMS

BREWING POTIONS

Potions give a variety of cool effects, so let's get brewing!

STEP ONE: ASSEMBLE YOUR INGREDIENTS

To brew your own potions, you'll need:
> One brewing stand, which you can take from an igloo basement or a church
> Three glass bottles, crafted from three glass blocks
> One Nether wart per potion, retrieved from the Nether (see Project #5)
> One blaze powder per brewing operation, also retrieved from the Nether
> A water source

You'll also need at least one primary potion ingredient from the following list: sugar, rabbit's foot, blaze powder, glistering melon, spider eye, ghast tear, magma cream, pufferfish, golden carrot, turtle shell and phantom membrane.

Plus, optionally, any potion modifier from this list: fermented spider eye, gunpowder, glowstone and dragon's breath.

Nether wart is the most essential ingredient, since without it you can only brew Potions of Weakness. This plant can be collected from fortresses in the Nether.

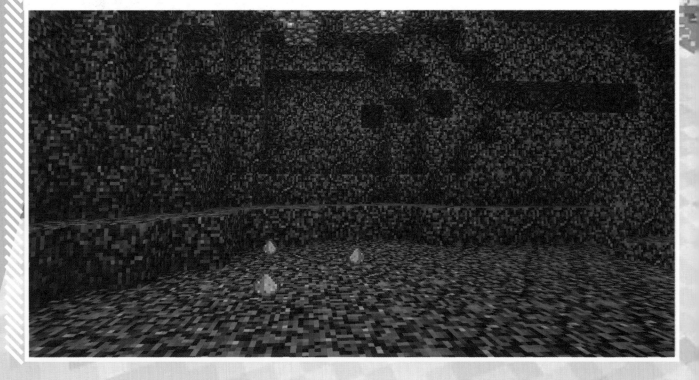

STEP TWO:
PREPARE

Place your brewing stand, then fill your three glass bottles with water. Place the water bottles in the output slots of the brewing stand's interface. At this point, you can add a fermented spider eye to make a Potion of Weakness, glowstone to make a (useless) thick potion, and other primary ingredients to make a (useless) mundane potion, gunpowder to make a splash water bottle, or Nether wart to make an awkward potion (this is the one to do!)

The first brewing operation will create three awkward potions and use up one blaze powder.

TIP: Blaze powder is crafted from blaze rods, dropped by blazes in the Nether. There's no other way to get them in Survival mode!

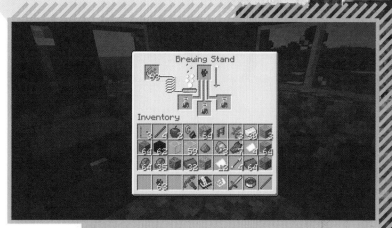

STEP THREE:
BASE POTIONS

Leave the awkward potions in the output slots of the brewing stand. You can now add a primary ingredient to create a useful potion.

Sugar makes a Potion of Swiftness, a rabbit's foot makes a Potion of Leaping, blaze powder makes a Potion of Strength, glistering melons make a Potion of Healing, spider eyes make a Potion of Poison, ghast tears make a Potion of Regeneration, magma cream makes a Potion of Fire Resistance, pufferfish make a Potion of Water Breathing, golden carrots make a Potion of Night Vision, turtle shells make a Potion of the Turtle Master, and phantom membranes make a Potion of Slow Falling. But that's not all!

PREPARE

STEP FOUR:
ADDED EXTRAS

You can add redstone dust to almost any potion to lengthen its effects. Alternatively, you can add glowstone to intensify its effects to Level II. Adding a fermented spider eye to certain potions corrupts their effects to create a new potion. You can make a Potion of Slowness, a Potion of Harming and a Potion of Invisibility this way.

Finally, you can add gunpowder to any potion to make it a throwable splash potion, and dragon's breath to any splash potion to make it a lingering potion, which stays on the ground when thrown (as pictured).

TIP: Drinking a bucket of milk instantly cures you of a status effect, even positive potion ones.

ADDED EXTRAS

TAMING MOBS

There aren't many friends to find in Minecraft, but these animals fit the bill!

WOLVES

Found in packs in forest and taiga biomes, you can tame a wolf by feeding it skeleton bones. Tamed wolves wear a collar, which you can dye different colours, and will attack enemies alongside you. If you feed a pair of tame wolves meat, they'll breed a baby wolf that's also tame.

HORSES / DONKEYS

Both equine mobs spawn in plains and savanna biomes. To tame them, you first have to "break" them by approaching with an empty hand and getting on their back until they stop throwing you off. Once they accept you as a rider, you can equip them with a saddle by opening the inventory while on their back. Donkeys can't wear armour, but carry chests, and if you breed a horse with a donkey you'll create a mule, which can wear armour AND carry a chest.

DOLPHINS

These ocean dwellers can't be permanently tamed, but if you feed a dolphin cod it will lead you to the nearest chest, whether that's a shipwreck or buried treasure. This will allow you to collect the loot inside! If you break that chest, then feed them again, they'll take you to the next closest one!

TIP: If you feed dolphins, they trust you more! They like raw salmon or raw cod for their dinner!

OCELOTS & CATS

Ocelots spawn in jungle biomes, while cats spawn in villages and witch huts. To gain their trust, stand still with an uncooked fish and wait for them to approach. When they get within three blocks, you can feed them. Do this enough times and they'll become tame. Tamed cats and ocelots can scare away creepers, and sometimes when you wake up a tame cat will gift you something it has collected overnight.

PARROTS

Available in five colours, parrots are found only in jungle biomes. You tame them by feeding them seeds, which causes them to fly behind you and even perch on your shoulder. They mimic the sounds of nearby mobs and will dance if music plays from a nearby jukebox.

LLAMAS

LLAMAS

Found in savanna and mountain biomes, llamas have four different skins and can be tamed the same way as horses. You can't saddle a llama, but you can decorate it with a carpet tile and equip it with a chest. If you attach a lead to a tamed llama, other llamas will follow it in a train of up to 10 animals! Their ability to carry items is determined by a hidden strength attribute, but will be between three and 15 items.

TIP: You tame llamas by feeding them either 10 wheat or 5 hay bales. They're hungry creatures, but after that, they'll be your friend!

DEFEAT THE PILLAGERS

Running into pillagers doesn't have to mean death...

OUTPOSTS

Pillager outposts are rare structures that spawn near villages. They're surrounded by smaller structures and filled with crossbow-carrying pillagers. The loot at the top of outposts is usually worth fighting your way up for. Be as stealth as possible, ensure you have strong weapons, and look out for any imprisoned iron golems. If you let them out of their cages, they'll fight the pillagers for you!

OUTPOSTS

PATROLS

Patrols consist of wandering pillagers and vindicators that spawn in groups of 2-5. They can spawn in any biome except Mushroom Fields. It's possible to avoid them, but if you get into a fight try to run across a river or into the sea, as water slows them down and you can pick them off from a distance. Defeating patrols is hard, and the rewards aren't very good, so trying to outrun them is the smartest choice!

PATROLS

CAPTAINS

A pillager carrying an illager banner is a captain. Killing a captain will result in you being given the Bad Omen effect for 100 minutes, or five in-game days, although you can remove this effect by drinking a bucket of milk. If you enter a village with the Bad Omen effect, you trigger a raid – and that's bad news for everyone...

TIP: Pillagers drop crossbows when they die, so make sure you check around for them after you've had a scrap with a patrol!

CAPTAINS

BEAT A RAID

Have you accidentally triggered a raid? We can help!

RAID CONDITIONS

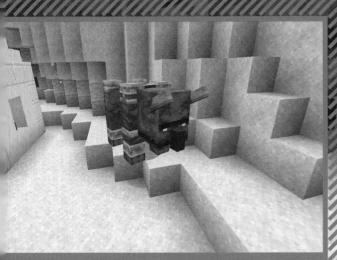
RAID TIPS

HERO OF THE VILLAGE

RAID CONDITIONS

If you enter a village with the Bad Omen effect, a raid will begin. The level of the effect determines how bad the raid is, with a Level 6 causing 10 waves of bad guys. When a raid starts, pillagers and vindicators will attack the village, occasionally joined by large, bull-like creatures called ravagers. To defeat the raid, you have to kill all of these enemies – something that's easier said than done...

RAID TIPS

Ringing a village's bell will apply a glowing outline to every hostile mob in a 32-block radius, and make villagers run to the safety of their home. Use this to keep track of who to take out!

Using a shield to block a ravager attack will make it roar, damaging nearby mobs, including illagers, some of whom may turn on the ravager. Far easier than killing it yourself!

Ravagers have 100 points of damage and are deadly to fight. The best thing to do is get up high where they can't attack you and shoot them from above with arrows.

HERO OF THE VILLAGE

If you beat the raid, you'll get the Hero of the Village status effect, which last for 60 minutes and gives you a discount of 30-55% from all members of that village, depending on the level of the effect. The higher the Bad Omen level, the higher the eventually Hero level when you win!

TIP: A raid contains a minimum of three waves, so don't be surprised if it takes some time to beat one!

SLAY THE

The ender dragon is the game's main boss. Here's how to fight it...

DRAGON

The ender dragon is the game's main boss. Here's how to fight it...

END CRYSTALS

When you enter the End, you'll spot large obsidian pillars with End crystals on top. These heal the dragon, so before you do anything it's a good idea to take them out. You may have to build to get high enough! If you can blow them up while the dragon is drawing energy from them, it will get hurt, too, so time your shots well. Make sure you're not too close when they explode, or you'll take damage as well!

TACTICS

The dragon has two main attack modes. In one, it flies around the island of the End and dives to attack. In another, it hovers in place and shoots dragon's breath at you. Try to hit it with arrows and avoid getting close, as its hits are painful! Remember to collect dragon's breath that lies on the ground in a glass bottle to make a lingering potion. There's no other way to get it!

SUMMON A NEW DRAGON

When you beat the dragon for the first time, you get 12,000 experience points and the exit portal will activate. You can summon a new dragon to fight, deactivating the portal, by placing one End crystal on each side of the portal. These are crafted from seven glass blocks, one eye of ender and one ghast tear. The second and all subsequent times you kill the dragon, you get only 500 experience points.

TIP: It IS possible to collect the dragon egg – you just need to find a way to make it fall onto a torch!

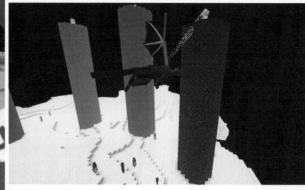
END CRYSTALS

TACTICS

SUMMON A NEW DRAGON

SUMMON THE WITHER

It's the hardest and scariest boss in Minecraft! Are you ready?

WHAT YOU NEED

WHAT HAPPENS NEXT

IF YOU WIN...

WHAT YOU NEED

You can summon a wither anywhere by placing four blocks of soul sand (or soul soil) in a T shape, then placing three wither skeleton skulls on top. Soul sand and soil are easy to find in the Nether, but to get wither skeleton skulls you have to kill around 120 wither skeletons, as the skull has only a one in 40 chance of dropping!

WHAT HAPPENS NEXT

When you build the wither's totem, it will appear in all white and begin to shake. Run away now! There's about to be a huge explosion that you don't want to get caught in. The wither is hostile to all mobs except zombies and skeletons, so try to attack it while it's distracted. Iron golems can't help much with this fight, but they can draw its fire off you! On Normal and Hard difficulty modes, the wither can inflict the Wither effect, which drains your hearts and turns them black, so you don't know how much health you have.

IF YOU WIN...

Killing the wither causes it to drop a Nether star, which you need to craft a beacon block. You can summon and kill a wither as many times as you like, but once is usually more than enough! The wither drops only 50 experience points despite its difficulty – if you want experience, go after the dragon instead!

TIP: The wither's skull attack leaves a wither rose on the ground whenever it kills another mob.

REACH THE NETHER

Ready to visit the Nether? It's time to take a trip to Minecraft's most punishing dimension...

STEP ONE: LOCATE OBSIDIAN

To visit the Nether, you need to build your first portal. It's actually not that difficult, it just requires a lot of leg work!

To build a portal, you need obsidian, which is formed when water flows over the top of still lava blocks. This means it naturally forms low down in many cave systems, where lava lakes are plentiful. The bottom of many ravines are also full of obsidian.

If you're feeling resourceful, you can mine obsidian most safely by making it yourself. Fill a bucket with water, look for a surface-level lava lake, then drop the water on top. Hey presto, you get some instant obsidian!

MINING OBSIDIAN

STEP TWO: MINE OBSIDIAN

Obsidian is super hard – in fact, it's the strongest destructible block in the game. It IS possible to break it with your bare hands, but it takes over four minutes of uninterrupted mining to do so. If you want to COLLECT obsidian, you'll need to use a diamond pickaxe.

Take care when mining: because of the way obsidian forms, it often sits on top of lava, so breaking the wrong block might mean it drops in and gets incinerated – or you do!

You need to collect a minimum of 10 blocks of obsidian to build a portal frame, or 14 if you want the frame to have corners.

TIP: Netherite pickaxes also mine obsidian, but you can't get those until you've been to the Nether!

STEP THREE: BUILD A PORTAL

You can build a Nether portal anywhere, but take care when you do as zombie piglins can come through from the other side. It's a good idea to place your portal somewhere safe and secure to make sure you don't get any nasty surprises!

To make a valid portal, it has to be built upright, as shown. The frame must be at least six blocks high by four blocks wide, and no more than 23 blocks high by 23 blocks wide. There can be no gaps in the frame, although if you're short on obsidian you can leave out the corners.

If you're really short on obsidian, find and restore a ruined portal. Simply fill in any gaps in the frame and replace any crying obsidian (it looks like obsidian with glowing, purple marks) with normal obsidian!

MAKING OBSIDIAN

STEP FOUR: ACTIVATE THE PORTAL

To activate the portal, simply set the interior of the frame on fire using a flint & steel, crafted out of an iron ingot and a piece of flint.

To deactivate a portal, you just have to break one of the obsidian blocks and it will switch off automatically.

Before you step into the portal, remember to stock up on food, armour, weapons and courage! Good luck...

TIP: Don't forget to plan for the return journey – take the right materials to build a portal back to the Overworld once you're done.

A RUINED PORTAL

THE NETHER:
AN EXPERT GUIDE

Once you step through that portal, it's a whole new world – literally!

REASONS TO VISIT

The Nether is a dangerous and terrifying place, so why should you visit at all? The loot you can collect in the Nether is great for crafting advanced items, and the landscape is made of material you can't get anywhere else.

In particular, look out for blaze rods and Nether wart, which are essential for brewing potions and crafting eyes of ender! Ghast tears and magma cream are rarer mob drops, but worth collecting if you can. And, of course, there's Netherite – the hardest material in the game!

STARTING A BASE

As soon as you enter the Nether, it makes sense to build a safe haven around your entry portal, to prepare your incursions and store your gear. Build a stone room around the portal and make sure you can see out.

Under NO circumstances should you place a bed in the Nether. It's impossible to respawn here, so if you try to sleep in a bed it will explode!

REASONS TO VISIT

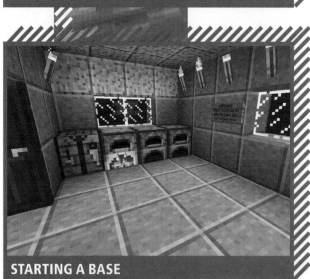
STARTING A BASE

FAST TRAVEL

The Nether has a strange relationship with the Overworld. Each block you travel in the Nether corresponds to eight blocks in the Overworld, so you can travel large distances in a fraction of the time if you walk a short distance then build a portal back to the Overworld. Creating portal networks is a great way to explore both dimensions – just remember to keep track of the route between them, because maps and compasses don't work in the Nether.

TIP: Enchanted golden apples are great fuel for any trip to the Nether, as they give you a Fire Resistance status effect when eaten!

FAST TRAVEL

WARPED FOREST

BASALT DELTA

NETHER BIOMES

There are five biomes in the Nether:

NETHER WASTE is mostly composed of Netherrack, gravel and soul sand. Look for quartz, Nether gold ore and ancient debris.

SOUL SAND VALLEY is tinted blue and filled with exposed fossils. It's a good place to find ghasts.

CRIMSON FOREST is a red fungal forest where piglins and hoglins reside. The amount of fungus growing here makes it good for collecting food.

WARPED FOREST is a denser, blue fungal forest. It's the safest part of the Nether, as only endermen and striders spawn here, so there are no openly hostile mobs.

BASALT DELTA is perhaps the most dangerous biome because it's uneven and full of lava. Bastion remnants never generate here.

NETHERITE

When you mine ancient debris with a diamond pickaxe or better, it drops as a block, which you can smelt into Netherite scrap. Craft together four Netherite scrap and four gold ingots to create a Netherite ingot. You can use a smithing table (*four wood planks and two iron ingots*) to upgrade any diamond gear with Netherite using one ingot.

Netherite Ingots can also be crafted into a block of Netherite, or you can craft a lodestone by surrounding one ingot with chiseled stone bricks. Lodestones are useful for "magnetising" a compass so it works in the Nether, meaning always pointing back to the lodestone. Put a lodestone by your main portal out of the Nether and you'll always be able to find it!

TIP: You can't place water in the Nether, but if you bring a cauldron and add water to it, you can put yourself out if you're on fire!

NETHER MOBS

PIGLINS

STRIDERS

NETHER MOBS

Most Nether mobs are fireproof, and they're all very strong! Try to avoid provoking zombified piglins and piglin brutes as they'll attack in groups and can quickly become overwhelming. Most mobs can survive in the Overworld if brought through using a portal (and vice versa!). But if you bring piglins or hoglins through to the Overworld, they'll become zombified after a short amount of time. The complete list of mobs you can encounter is: blazes, endermen, ghasts, hoglins, magma cubes, piglins, piglin brutes, skeletons, striders, wither skeletons and zombified piglins.

PIGLINS & BARTERING

Piglins are fond of gold, and if you give them a gold ingot they'll repay you with a random item from this list: obsidian, crying obsidian, fire charge, Nether brick, spectral arrow, gravel, blackstone, string, Nether quartz, water bottle, iron nugget, ender pearl, iron boots with Soul Speed enchantment, splash Potion of Fire Resistance, Potion of Fire Resistance and enchanted book (Soul Speed). Note that piglin babies and piglin brutes (the ones that carry axes) will not barter with you.

STRIDERS

The only rideable mob in the Nether, striders spawn on lava (usually in lava oceans) and have a one in 30 chance of spawning with a piglin rider and saddle. Striders can walk on lava, and if you sit on a saddled one it can be directed using a warped fungus on a stick (crafted from a fishing rod and warped fungus). They become cold if they're not on lava, turning blue and shivering. You can breed them by feeding two adults a warped fungus each.

TIP: When bartering, the most common item (obsidian) is given nine in 100 trades, while the least common, the enchanted book, occurs just one in 100 trades.

BASTION REMNANTS

BASTION REMNANTS

These half-demolished ruins are the remains of large castles built by hoglins. They can occur in almost any Nether biome except the Basalt Delta and are made entirely of blackstone, which is a variant of cobblestone native to the Nether. They sometimes contain Nether wart farms, but the thing to look for are the chests, which contain rare and enchanted gear. Watch out for piglin brutes and hoglins, as well as lava!

FORTRESSES

Found in any biome, Nether fortresses are large, sprawling structures made almost entirely of Nether bricks. They're composed of huge walkways that usually tower above the ground, and sets of dungeons and corridors, which are often embedded in the landscape. You can find lots of good loot and Nether wart, but beware the mobs that spawn here. Blazes and wither skeletons will only appear in fortresses, but if you want to get the best gear from the Nether you'll have to pay them a visit.

FORTRESSES

RUINED PORTALS

These shattered remains of Nether portals generate in both the Nether and the Overworld, and you can repair them to travel back and forth between the dimensions – ideal if you get stuck in the Nether without any obsidian! They all have a loot chest near them, which you can use to collect enchanted gear. They can generate virtually anywhere in either dimension, so keep an eye out for them as you never know when they'll come in handy.

TIP: Hoglins also turn into zombies outside the Nether. In this state, they're known as zoglins!

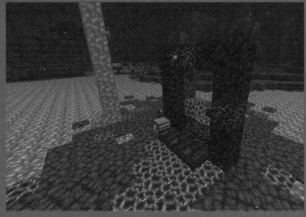

RUINED PORTALS

THE END:
AN EXPERT GUIDE

Once you've survived a stronghold, there's only one place left to go!

ACTIVATING THE PORTAL

If you've read our guide to strongholds, you'll know each one contains a portal room. These are different to Nether portals. To activate them, you have to insert an eye of ender into each block of the portal frame. There are 12 blocks in total, and some are usually already filled in, so 12 eyes should be more than enough. Once you insert all of them, the portal will spring to life, and when you enter you'll find yourself in the End...

BEAT THE DRAGON

The first thing to do is beat the dragon. Again, there's a guide on that elsewhere in this book! Once you do this, you'll gain access to the further reaches of the End via End gateways. The only way out is to die or use the exit portal, but once you've beaten the dragon you can cross back and forth without having to fight again, so replenish your health and stock up before you use an End gateway!

ACTIVATING THE PORTAL

BEAT THE DRAGON

END GATEWAYS

These gateways are small, floating portals that appear in the void around the edges of the island you arrive on once you beat the dragon. Each time you defeat the dragon, a new gateway will spawn. You can travel through them by throwing ender pearls into them, and when you do you'll be transported to the distant reaches of the End.

TIP: End portals are activated permanently – unlike Nether portals, they can't be switched off, even if you break the frames in Creative mode.

END GATEWAYS

THE LANDSCAPE

When you arrive in the End, you'll spawn on the central island, which is a large, floating piece of rock surrounded by a seemingly endless void. Once you pass through a gateway, you'll be teleported hundreds of blocks away to the outer islands, which surround the central island at a great distance. Each island varies in size, and crossing between them is best achieved using ender pearls to teleport yourself. There are very few types of block in this dimension – it's mostly just End stone as far as the eye can see!

CHORUS PLANTS

The large, twisting purple structures you see in the outer islands are called chorus plants. They can be grown on End stone and produce chorus flowers and chorus fruit. If you break the bottom of a chorus plant, all blocks connected to it will also fall, making it easy to harvest. You get 0-1 chorus fruit per plant when you do this.

CHORUS FRUIT

Chorus fruit is the only source of food in the Nether. When you eat one, you regain a little health, but also get teleported a few blocks away in a random direction, so make sure you don't accidentally teleport yourself into the void! If you smelt a chorus fruit, it turns into a popped chorus fruit, which is inedible but can be used to craft purpur blocks (*four popped fruit*) or an End rod (*one popped fruit and a blaze rod*).

TIP: Chorus fruit teleportation effects have a range of eight blocks in any direction, but will only teleport you into empty spaces.

THE LANDSCAPE

CHORUS PLANTS

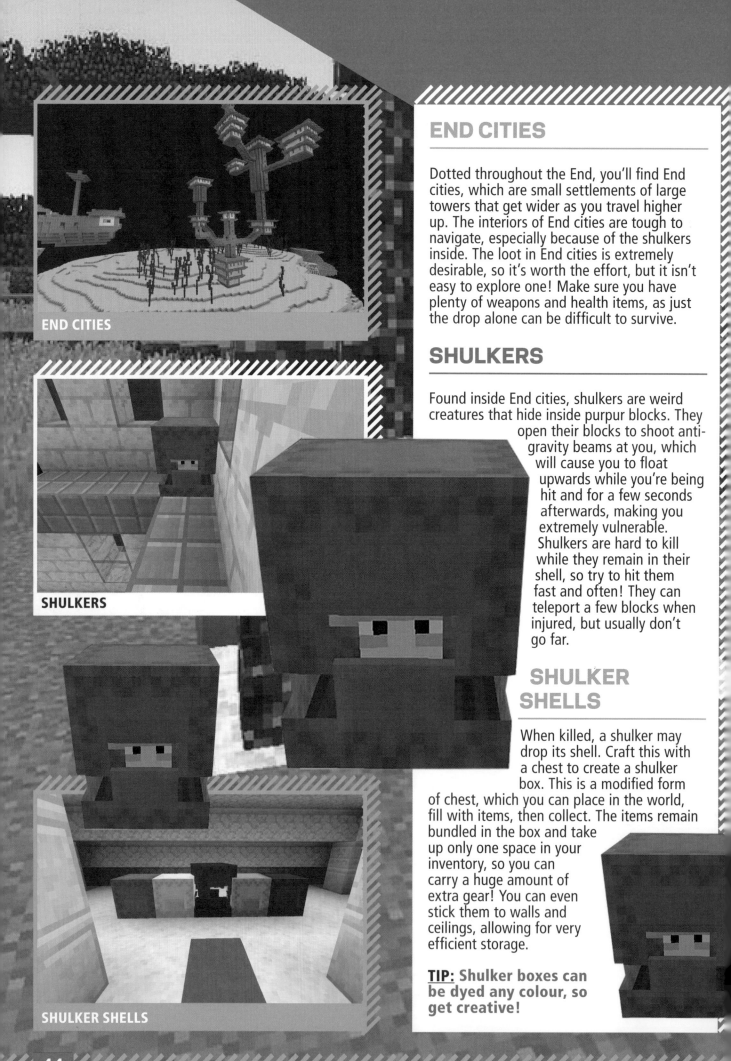

END CITIES

Dotted throughout the End, you'll find End cities, which are small settlements of large towers that get wider as you travel higher up. The interiors of End cities are tough to navigate, especially because of the shulkers inside. The loot in End cities is extremely desirable, so it's worth the effort, but it isn't easy to explore one! Make sure you have plenty of weapons and health items, as just the drop alone can be difficult to survive.

SHULKERS

Found inside End cities, shulkers are weird creatures that hide inside purpur blocks. They open their blocks to shoot anti-gravity beams at you, which will cause you to float upwards while you're being hit and for a few seconds afterwards, making you extremely vulnerable. Shulkers are hard to kill while they remain in their shell, so try to hit them fast and often! They can teleport a few blocks when injured, but usually don't go far.

SHULKER SHELLS

When killed, a shulker may drop its shell. Craft this with a chest to create a shulker box. This is a modified form of chest, which you can place in the world, fill with items, then collect. The items remain bundled in the box and take up only one space in your inventory, so you can carry a huge amount of extra gear! You can even stick them to walls and ceilings, allowing for very efficient storage.

TIP: Shulker boxes can be dyed any colour, so get creative!

END CITIES

SHULKERS

SHULKER SHELLS

END SHIPS

Around half of all End cities have a floating End ship connected to them. Don't leave the End until you've raided one! The only bad guys inside are shulkers, and they contain some fantastic loot, including enchanted gear and armour, plus – in an item frame in the hold – a pair of elytra!

ELYTRA

The elytra is named after insect forewings, and worn in the armour chestplate slot. It gives you the ability to glide by pressing jump in mid-air. You can even set off firework rockets while travelling to give yourself a boost, allowing you to soar above the world. When damaged, you can repair the elytra using phantom membranes, collected from the phantom mob that sometimes attacks you in the Overworld if you haven't slept for several in-game days. It's perhaps the rarest item in the game, and certainly one of the hardest to get! If you've bagged yourself a pair of elytra without cheating, you can truly say you've beaten Minecraft.

DRAGON HEADS

At the front of every End ship, you'll spot a figurehead – the dragon head. This double-sized block can be worn as a mask or placed on the wall as a trophy.

For a laugh, you can even connect redstone power up to it, to make the mouth open and close! Remember to snag it whenever you find an End ship – it's mostly decorative, but fantastic fun.

TIP: Once the elytra's durability is used up, it isn't destroyed completely, but must be repaired before it will fly again. Just try not to let that happen in mid-air!

END SHIPS

ELYTRA

DRAGON HEAD

LIGHTING A BEACON

Proof that you've mastered Minecraft, beacons are also great fun to make!

STEP ONE:
GETTING WHAT YOU NEED

Most of the components for a beacon are easy to get hold of – it's only the beacon block itself that's hard to obtain!

To start with, you need to collect a huge amount of resource materials. Beacons are made up of blocks of iron, gold, Netherite, emerald and diamond. You can use all five types interchangeably, but each block needs nine units of material, and you need a minimum of nine blocks (81 materials) to make a beacon. The

biggest beacons need 164 blocks – that's 1,476 materials!

But that's nowhere near as tough as collecting the Nether star you need to make the beacon block. You have to summon, survive and kill the wither! After that, it's easy – just craft together three obsidian, five glass blocks and the Nether star.

STEP TWO: BUILDING THE BASE

The smallest beacon is created by putting a beacon block in the centre of a 3x3 platform made of valid resource blocks. This is a one-level beacon. If you build a 5x5 platform with a 3x3 platform on top, and a beacon block on that, you have a two-level beacon. The largest beacon is four levels with a 9x9 base.

Adding levels to your beacon improves its status buffs and extends its range. At one level, the beacon casts its effect over 20 blocks; at four levels, this extends to 50 blocks.

TIP: There's no penalty for mixing and matching types of block, and no reward for using the rarest – it can just look neater if you stick to one type.

STEP TWO

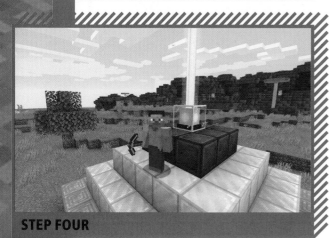

STEP FOUR

STEP THREE: POWERING THE BEACON

To activate a beacon, the beacon block has to be under open sky. Use the beacon block and you'll see the interface. Charge the beacon block by putting a gold, Netherite or iron ingot, diamond or emerald in the main slot. This will allow you to select a status buff above, and a secondary status buff if you have a large enough beacon. This charges the beacon and causes it to fire a tall, white beam into the sky.

STEP FOUR: STATUS BUFFS

Once a beacon is charged and activated, it will begin granting one of five main status buffs:
➤ One-level beacons can grant Speed I, which increases movement, or Haste I, which increases mining/attack speed.
➤ Two-level beacons can offer (in addition to Speed and Haste) the Resistance I effect, which decreases damage, and Jump Boost I, which increases jump height.
➤ Three-level beacons can also grant Strength I, which increases melee damage.
➤ Four-level beacons can grant a Level II version of any of these status buffs. They can also pair this buff with Regeneration I, which regenerates your health if you're close by!

TIP: You can change the colour of a beacon's beam by putting a stained glass block above it.

BUILD
SPOTLIGHT

Looking for inspiration for your next project? Check out these fantastic recreations!

> Midtown Manhattan by BasVerhagen is a great recreation of New York City's most thriving district, all accomplished within Minecraft! **www.planetminecraft.com/ project/midtown-manhattan/**

> Aerowin by TheChriZ1995 gives you a full-size cruise ship to play around in, whether you want to explore alone or with your friends! **www.planetminecraft.com/project/ aerowin-cruise-liner/**

> Serenity by MrFruitTree is a perfect recreation of a modern house, all of which fits into a 16x16 block chunk.
www.planetminecraft.com/project/ serenity-1349110/

> Modern Café by Nefashus is a great addition to any city build, showcasing a modern-style café-restaurant.
www.planetminecraft.com/project/ nefas-modern-caf/